PHYSICIAN MANAGERS
AND THE LAW

Legal Aspects of Medical Quality Management

Edited by James B. Couch, MD, JD

The American College
of Physician Executives

One Urban Centre
Suite 648
4830 West Kennedy Boulevard
Tampa, Florida 33609-2517
813/287-2000

Copyright © 1989 by the American College of Physician Executives. All rights reserved. Reproduction or translation of this work beyond that permitted by applicable copyright law without permission of the publisher is prohibited. Requests for permission to reprint or for further information should be directed to ACPE, One Urban Centre, Suite 648, 4830 West Kennedy Blvd., Tampa, Florida 33609-2517.

"This publication is designed to provide accurate and authoritative information in regard to the subject matter covered. It is sold with the understanding that the publisher is not engaged in rendering legal, accounting, or other professional service. If legal advice or other expert assistance is required, the services of a competent professional should be sought." *From a Declaration of Principles jointly adopted by a committee of the American Bar Association and a Committee of Publishers.*

ISBN: 0-924674-01-6

Printed in the United States of America
by Lithocolor Printing Corp., Tampa, Florida

Foreword

It is now a year since the American College of Physician Executives created its Societies and Forums. What has been gratifying in that year has been the speed and clarity with which the Societies and Forums have fulfilled the expectations of the College Board of Directors. Our educational programming has been improved immeasurably by the infusion of the new ideas and enthusiastic direction of the Societies and Forums. And now we have the first publication from these important components of the College's drive to increase the influence of physician executives in the policy-making bodies of government and other health care organizations.

This monograph has an especially interesting background, having been produced through the cooperative efforts of two of our Forums--Law and Medicine and Quality Health Care. Its editor, James B. Couch, MD, JD, is Cochair of the Forum on Law and Medicine and has a special and abiding interest in medical quality management. Prior to his efforts as editor and author for this monograph, Dr. Couch wrote a series of three monographs for the College entitled *Medical Quality Management for Physician Executives in the 1990s*. Now, with the assistance of colleagues on the Forum on Law and Medicine and the Forum on Quality Health Care, he has helped to produce a study of the legal aspects of medical quality management. We are confident that this volume will join our other medical quality management monographs and our series on Physician Managers and the Law as a basic text for physician executives. We are proud to have played a part with Dr. Couch and his coauthors in bringing the project to fruition. And we eagerly await the publications that are certain to come from the Societies and Forums in the years ahead.

Roger Schenke
Executive Vice President
American College of Physician Executives
Tampa, Florida
May 1, 1989

Introduction

In this very special monograph, James B. Couch, MD, JD, has constructed a unique perspective for physician executives on legal issues related to the profound changes now under way in health care. This publication called upon members active in the Forums on Law and Medicine and Quality Health Care who also have extensive legal, administrative, and professional involvements in the rapidly emerging field of medical quality management. The monograph provides an informative and timely commentary on issues that will become increasingly more relevant to all physicians, especially those involved in managing health care services.

The legal and medical professions share much in common with regard to general commitment to quality in health care. Few would argue that quality--measured in terms of accessibility, service, technical sophistication, comprehensiveness, and efficacy in delivery--has emerged as one of the popularly derived "rights" in American society. To achieve high-quality services, health professionals must constantly maintain proficiency of knowledge and skills. They must also become more knowledgeable about "systems" issues relevant to their making clinical decision affecting the quality of medical interventions:

- Organizational and psychosocial aspects of treatment and healing.

- Cost implications of clinical decisions made compositely by multiple health professionals over time in achieving a positive longitudinal health status for the patient.

- "Professional" determinants in quality--standards, credentials, ethics.

- Legal parameters for quality, as established by laws, regulations, legal determinations, administrative policies, and contracts.

Physician executives have a special responsibility and accountability in achieving quality improvement goals. It could be argued that their minds, desks, and files represent the omnibus of quality in the health care encounter. Physician executives must anticipate, arbitrate, lead, analyze, and advocate in moving their organizations toward quality goals that at once must be legally, financially, and clinically sound. This multidimensional "tall order" will require ever-increasing knowledge of developments in areas affecting the effective management of their programs--including health law, legislation, and quality measurement and improvement systems.

The American College of Physician Executives, through its Societies and Forums, will be providing a diverse and relevant array of educational services to assist medical managers in meeting the multiple demands of patients, payers, governments, courts, and other parties for high-quality health care. This monograph represents an important contribution to the College's commitment to the education of its members and the public. It should be read thoroughly and referenced often. And it should serve as a foundation for the many future College publications, seminars, and other educational offerings related to the legal aspects of quality. These efforts will increasingly establish the American College of Physician Executives as a national resource for the enlarging focus on quality in health care.

Alex R. Rodriguez, MD, FACPE
Chair, Forum on Quality Health Care
American College of Physician Executives
May 1, 1989

Contents

Foreword i

Introduction ii

Chapter One 1
Recent Legal Developments in the Medical
   Quality Management Field
Nigel Roberts, MD, and Norman M. Charney, MD, JD

Chapter Two 11
The Medical Staff and Quality Assurance
Dale H. Cowan, MD

Chapter Three 15
Guidelines for Medical Quality Management
   Program Development
Edward H. Lipson, MD, MS, FACPE

Chapter Four 24
Legal Aspects of Physician Credentialing
Todd Sagin, MD, JD

Chapter Five 38
Legal Aspects of Clinical Outcome Management
James B. Couch, MD, JD, and Alex R. Rodriguez, MD, FACPE

Chapter Six 48
Physician Executives as Medical Systems Experts
James B. Couch, MD, JD

Chapter Seven 52
Epilogue
James B. Couch, MD, JD

Index 54

Chapter One

Recent Legal Developments in the Medical Quality Management Field

by Nigel Roberts, MD,
and Norman M. Charney, MD, JD

Introduction

The management of medical quality has become one of the most challenging aspects of the delivery of health care as we enter the 1990s. For the physician manager, these times are most exciting, because there has never been such a focus from so many varied sources on a single aspect of health care. In this chapter we are going to refer to four such sources:

- Statutory and regulatory developments.

- "Voluntary" professional initiatives.

- Academic initiatives.

- Judicial developments.

Rather than describe each of these areas fully and in isolation, their actual and anticipated effects on physician executives are described. The field of medical quality management is advancing rapidly and is really the ultimate product of the integration of the disparate forces cited above. This chapter will touch upon the most recent examples of these forces.

Furthermore, we appreciate that, with so many "sources" of change, one federal or state legislative effort may alter the scenarios, as could any initiative, finding, or judgment. Nevertheless, there continues to be an inexorable movement toward assessment and assurance of quality in health care services delivery.

Whether one subscribes to the theory of the "bad apple" or to the theory of continuous quality improvement,[1] the goals of those interested in the field are similar. The simple goal is to improve the quality of care.

The desire to improve the quality of care assumes a lot. It assumes that one can define, assess, and assure quality. To assess quality, one must be intimately familiar with the clinical decision-making process. To strive for a high-quality outcome for a medical process or for a treatment strategy implies that the clinical decision-making process is not only intact but also correct.

That is precisely the importance of clinical research and of the initiatives of various national medical specialty societies, such as the American College of Physicians. The realization that the field of medicine is fluid must be factored into any quest for quality. Inherent in clinical decision-making are judgments of medical necessity and appropriateness and of efficiency and recognition of inappropriateness, profligate spending, and system abuse. Who would have thought that the life-saving or life-extending procedure of coronary artery bypass surgery may be performed inappropriately as much as 44 percent of the time?[2] Who would have thought that the apparently obvious benefit of pulmonary artery catheter in patients with acute myocardial infarction would be questioned? Yet the practice was not only questioned but also linked to as many as 16,000 deaths, resulting in a moratorium being called on its placement.[3]

These examples should not dismissed and taken as too specific. They should be regarded as acknowledgments that the field of medicine is excitingly changing and that any system that we build for the attainment of quality must be flexible enough to cope rationally with new knowledge and information.

Because this monograph is directed primarily to physician executives, emphasis is placed on the evolution of medical quality management as it affects the physician executive. The first part of this chapter will cite recent examples of statutory, regulatory, voluntary, academic, and professional initiatives addressing some of the most important issues currently affecting the medical quality management field from legal, managerial, and public policy perspectives.

Physician Credentialing

Physician credentialing is an elemental part of medical quality management. It is part of the *structure* of any such system. Even a review of whether or not an individual person practicing medicine is a licensed physician is a beginning. In most states a small percentage of physicians have lost their licenses, have let them expire, or even are using them fraudulently. Generally, the state boards of licensure will have records, but they do not communicate this information in any consistent fashion to other states. Indeed it is not unusual for a physician to take up residence and practice in another state after some disciplinary action has occurred.

As medical care organizations become multistate operations, their databases may provide more information about disciplined physicians. In recognition of current communication gaps among state licensing boards concerning physician discipline, the Health Care Quality Improvement Act of 1986 (P.L. 99-660) provides for a National Practitioner Data Bank, which may link in one central repository the information from the several states. It also provides ground rules for reporting of and access to the information. It lays out due process safeguards and affords antitrust immunity to hospitals, peer review bodies and those assisting those bodies for compliance with its data reporting requirements, and substantive and procedural safeguards in the review of physicians' clinical performance in the context of its credentialing functions.

To retain federal antitrust immunity, hospitals must access information from the data bank on all physicians applying for appointment and reappointment to their medical staffs. Failure to do so will result in loss of this immunity for a period of three years. Independent proof of this failure also will permit a plaintiff's attorney to access the data bank for information about a defendant physician in an action against the hospital. The action will allege that had the hospital been aware of this physician's record of substandard practice, it should have restricted the physician's privileges to perform the allegedly negligent procedure or practice.

Reporting and access requirements regarding staff physicians' and physician applicants' disciplinary histories (including licensure and clinical privileges restrictions, professional society membership suspension for causes other than nonpayment of dues, and malpractice settlements and verdicts) will go into effect when the National Practitioner Data Bank becomes operational. Unisys, Inc., which as the successful contractor will function as the data bank for the Health Resources Services Administration, anticipates operations will start by the fall of 1989.

States such as California have worked to coordinate state law with this federal statute. In 1987, S.B. 1620 and A.B. 2249 were passed in California to go into effect on January 1, 1988. Essentially, the two laws expanded the state's peer review reporting requirements. The provisions now apply to most organized health care delivery settings, including medical groups of 25 or more professionals that have peer review processes in place. Any privilege restriction for medical disciplinary cause requires that a specific report be filed. In return for compliance with the state's law, there is reciprocal access to the state's data bank.

Medical Quality Monitoring and Evaluation

The *process* of delivery of health care clearly affects medical quality. Voluntary organizations such as the Joint Commission on Accreditation of Healthcare Organizations (JCAHO) have for a number of years focused on the structure and process of the health care delivery system in the hospital setting to assure quality. They have successfully nudged most acute care hospitals into beginning to understand that structural and procedural efforts need to be expanded to enhance or maintain quality. Since the early days of the Medicare program in the 1960s, hospitals' compliance with the Joint Commission's standards has been accepted by the Health Care Financing Administration (HCFA) as evidence of their satisfaction of the Medicare "Conditions of Participation."

The near universal hospital accreditation that currently occurs, however, makes additional criteria necessary for most payer organizations that wish to develop a preferred or select network of hospitals. Recognizing this, the JCAHO has recently approved a major policy change that will identify those 8 to 10 percent of the 5,300 hospitals the JCAHO accredits that are only "conditionally accredited." These hospitals will have six months to come into compliance. In the interim, "conditionally accredited" hospitals may well prove to be corporate liability "time bombs" (see discussion of corporate liability in the "judicial" section later in this chapter). Also, recognizing the strong movement toward clinical outcome assessment, the JCAHO intends to implement its own outcome assessment accreditation process in the 1990s known as the "Agenda for Change." A thorough analysis of the JCAHO outcome measurement system is outside the scope of this chapter but is available.[4,5]

State Regulations

In states where there are specific departmental responsibilities for licensing and regulating medical care organizations such as health maintenance organizations (HMOs), it is doubtful that the JCAHO accreditation process is as thorough or as far-reaching or could carry the authority of a state law enforcement agency. For instance, in California the Department of Corporations has the licensing and regulatory authority for HMOs. That authority specifically calls for assessment of the quality of care delivered, the quality assurance program, access to care, the grievance system, and a whole host of other areas, such as finance, the law, ownership, etc. As is fairly well known, the New York Department of Health, which enforces a "beefed up" version of the JCAHO standards, has recently proposed to quit reimbursing hospitals for JCAHO survey costs, believing such surveys are superfluous in light of its own stricter and more vigilantly enforced regulatory standards.

Federal Regulatory Initiatives

The Health Care Financing Administration's release of hospital-specific mortality data also has focused attention on outcome measurement as an indicator of quality. The data release itself is intended to provide an impetus to self-review and thus potentially to an improvement in quality.

Previously, the Tax Equity and Fiscal Responsibility Act of 1982 (TEFRA), which spawned the Peer Review Improvement Act, gave statutory authority to the peer review organizations (PROs) for the Medicare program, among other provisions. However, the PROs became primarily utilization review organizations. It was the fear that PROs were concentrating on cost containment at the expense of quality that gave rise to federal initiatives such as the annual HCFA mortality data release and the Omnibus Budget Reconciliation Act of 1986 (OBRA). This legislation refined the role of the PROs and conferred upon them responsibility for quality review. The act specifically outlines "improving quality of care with respect to (Medicare) Part A Services" and under the section Improved Review of Quality by Peer Review Organizations has specific provisions.

Notwithstanding the above federal statutes, the individual states, through the U.S. Constitution, have responsibility for the health, safety, and morals of the people. They have manifested this responsibility most recently through the growing establishment of state data commissions (for example, in Pennsylvania), which intend to release data to consumers and purchasers on the severity-of-illness-adjusted comparative costs and quality of care given by their state's health care providers.[6]

Academic and Professional Organizations

Academic and professional organizations have individually or jointly studied outcome as a measure of quality. The products of the (often federally funded) studies are beginning to affect the field of medical quality management. Below are identified some examples of completed studies and proposed ventures. The Codman Research Group headed by John Wennberg, MD, has identified geographic variations in the performance of procedures. The RAND/UCLA group has reported on appropriateness of certain costly invasive procedures. There is currently a tentative proposal from the American Medical Association and the RAND/UCLA group to apply for HCFA funding to develop clinical practice parameters for a wide variety of disease entities (see Chapter Five for details). Various private organizations are also becoming involved in far-ranging quality of care initiatives, including those involving refined outcome measurements, the Medicare Risk Contracts for HMOs, the Medicare PPO pilot demonstration program, and the coronary artery bypass graft center of excellence program.

The second part of this chapter will provide an elucidation of how the judiciary has created potential medical quality management liability pitfalls for physician executives.

Medical Quality Management Pitfalls

In a major opinion on a pornography case, U.S. Supreme Court Justice Potter Stewart said that while he did not know how to define pornography, he knew it when he saw it. The same might be said for medical quality. It has always been difficult to define, but everyone knows it when they see it.

Is medical quality truly in the eye of the beholder? Is medical quality as perceived by physicians the same as that perceived by patients?

Patients often think of medical quality in terms of the presence or absence of amenities, such as the cleanliness of the office, the length of the wait, or the courtesy of the staff. Physicians, on the other hand, may look at how correct the diagnosis was and how scientifically rigorous the treatment plan was. Other groups associated with health care delivery and its finances have perceptions completely different from these.[7]

Quality is elusive. Therefore, the appraisal of quality may be perceived as arbitrary and capricious. This may create the potential for litigation. Medical quality management may occur in various settings:

- Hospital medical groups.
- Independent practice associations (IPAs).
- Health maintenance organizations (HMOs).
- Preferred provider organizations (PPOs).
- Exclusive provider organizations (EPOs).
- Regulatory and accreditation agencies (for example, HCFA and JCAHO, respectively).
- Insurance companies and insurer/provider organizations (IPOs), such as EQUICOR, Inc.
- Hospitals and multi-institutional health care systems.

The second part of this chapter is intended to chart some of the judicial decisions affecting physician executives involved in medical quality management. This will be expanded in Chapter Four of the monograph, particularly as these judicial initiatives affect physician credentialing.

Liability Areas for Physician Executives

Physician executives may have varying exposure to medical quality management liability. If physician executives provide no "hands on" patient care, their liability still could be of a vicarious nature. An entity is vicariously liable (that is, legally responsible for the acts of another person) when a special relationship exists between the two entities.

Under the doctrine of *respondeat superior*, an employer is held vicariously liable for the negligent act of an employee who is acting within the scope of his or her employment. If the negligent party is considered an independent contractor, the doctrine does not apply.

In order for a physician executive to be held legally liable under the doctrine of vicarious liability for the acts of a negligent party, an employer/employee relationship or a closely analogous relationship must exist.

Physicians and nurses used to be viewed as independent contractors for whose acts the hospital was not liable. The hospital was perceived as merely furnishing the location where patients received care and treatment. It was not regarded as possessing any control over physicians and therefore could not be held responsible for their acts.

With the landmark decision *Darling v. Charleston Community Hospital*, 33 Ill 2nd 326, 111 NE 253 (1965), the Supreme Court of Illinois recognized that hospitals have a duty to assure the quality of care received by patients treated by physicians using their facilities.

There followed a host of other cases, including *Elam v. College Park*, 4 Cir. No. 24479 (Cal Ct. App.) (1982) and *Corleto v. Shore Memorial Hospital* 138 N.J. Sup 203350 A 2nd 554 (1975), the latter actually holding potentially accountable all 143 members of a medical staff because of inadequate oversight and restriction of clinical privileges of a habitually negligent staff member.

This concept of corporate liability may well extend in the 1990s to include health care regulatory agencies, insurance companies with managed care products, and any entity that is involved with medical quality management activities.

Wickline v. State of California, 183 Cal App 3rd 1175, 228 Cal Reptr 661, is a case in point. A Medi-Cal (Medicaid) reviewer granted a length of stay that the attending physician believed was inadequate. Nevertheless, he complied and discharged the patient from the hospital within the suggested timeframe. As a consequence, arterial blockage occurred, necessitating a subtotal leg amputation.

The Medi-Cal reviewer was charged with negligent abandonment, with the State of California as the vicariously liable entity. The plaintiff was awarded $500,000 at the trial court level. On appeal, the verdict was reversed merely on the grounds that the attending physician did not dispute the reviewer's ruling. However, it did establish that "third party-payers can be held legally accountable when medically inappropriate decisions result from defects in the design or implementation of cost containment programs."

HMOs may be subject to similar liability by virtue of their contractual arrangements with providers and their degree of utilization control.[8] In the staff model HMO, where all the providers are employed directly by the HMO, the liability flows by virtue of the employment relationship. In IPA and group model HMOs, the relationship is less clear. It will be the degree of control that the HMO assumes in the decision making that will determine whether an independent contractor relationship or the *respondeat superior* doctrine would apply. In addition, physician executives responsible for medical quality management in HMOs could be found liable along with the managed care system for inadequate quality assurance as described in the Darling case.

Institutional (as well as managerial) liability may also attach under the agency theory. Despite the fact that a negligent physician may not have been an agent of the corporate entity a physician executive may have been managing, there may be a misperception that such a negligent party was an agent. This is known as apparent agency.

Analogously, an entity such as an HMO creates an appearance to a patient that an agency relationship exists between the entity and physician providers. If the patient reasonably relies upon that appearance to his detriment or injury, liability may be created through the apparent agency theory of liability.

Other theories of liability may exist for the physician executive involved in medical quality management. These include negligent selection of providers and negligent control of utilization.

Contractual Liability in Medical Quality Management

The last area concerns contractual liability. Patients who are covered by insurance or health benefit plans sponsored by their employers are considered third-party beneficiaries. Even though the contract is between the insurance companies and the employer, it is considered to be for the benefit of the employee, that is, the third-party beneficiary. For example, an employee may even have standing in a contract action against an independent utilization reviewer whose actions directly or indirectly result in injury to the employee, despite the fact that the contractual relationship is between the reviewer and the insurance company. Furthermore, denial of coverage may lead to denial of care, because without the insurance benefit, the patient may not be able to afford the care. This can result in a compensable loss due to physical injuries as a consequence of lack of treatment.

Summary

The second half of this chapter has attempted to present a brief review of the potential legal consequences of medical quality management activities in which physician executives are and will be increasingly involved. Considerably more detail concerning how to manage these legal obstacles may be found in Chapter Four of this monograph and elsewhere.[7]

References

1. Berwick, D. "Continuous Improvement as an Ideal in Health Care." *New England Journal of Medicine* 320(1):53-6, Jan. 5, 1989.

2. Winslow, C., and others. "The Appropriateness of Performing Coronary Artery Bypass Surgery." *JAMA* 260(4):505-9, July 22, 1988.

3. Robin, E. "Death by Pulmonary Artery Flow-Directed Catheter: Time for a Moratorium?" *Chest* 92(6):727-31, Dec. 1987.

4. Couch, J. *Medical Quality Management for Physician Executives in the 1990s: Preparing for the Joint Commission's New Initiatives*. Tampa, Fla.: American College of Physician Executives, 1988.

5. Couch, J. "The Joint Commission on Accreditation of Healthcare Organizations" in *Providing Quality Care: The Challenge to Clinicians*. Philadelphia, Pa.: American College of Physicians, 1989.

6. Couch, J. *Medical Quality Management for Physician Executives in the 1990s: The Era of Medical Care Value Purchasing*. Tampa, Fla.: American College of Physician Executives, 1989.

7. Couch, J. *Medical Quality Management for Physician Executives in the 1990s: The Essentials of Medical Quality Management*. Tampa, Fla.: American College of Physician Executives, 1988.

8. Couch, J. "The Role of HMO Medical Directors in Contractual Negotiations" in *Physician Managers and the Law: Employment and Personal Services Contracts*. Tampa, Fla.: American College of Physician Executives, 1987.

Nigel Roberts, MD, is Associate Clinical Professor, School of Medicine, University of California at Los Angeles. He is a member of the College's Forum on Quality Health Care. Norman M. Charney, MD, JD, is California Medical Director for Coordinated Healthcare Systems, EQUICOR, San Diego, California. He is a member of the College's Forum on Law and Medicine.

Chapter Two

The Medical Staff and Quality Assurance

by Dale H. Cowan, MD

This chapter is intended to provide a concise discussion of how the medical staff is organized to accomplish its quality assurance functions, which are covered in more detail in Chapter Three of this monograph.

Standards of the Joint Commission on Accreditation of Healthcare Organizations (JCAHO) and most state hospital licensing statutes provide that the medical staff is the unit that has primary responsibility for the quality of care provided in the hospital. This chapter discusses the nature of the medical staff and the medical staff's responsibility for quality assurance.

The Structure of the Medical Staff

Medical staffs are organizations of physicians, and where authorized by state statutes, dentists, podiatrists, and other allied health professionals, who may provide clinical services in hospitals. The JCAHO specifies that each hospital has "...a single organized medical staff that has overall responsibility for accounting therefore to the governing body."[1]

A debate exists regarding the legal status of medical staffs. The traditional view is that the medical staff is a part of the hospital and constitutes an organizational unit within the hospital much like other hospital departments. According to this view, the medical staff has no existence apart from the hospital and therefore is not a separate legal entity. Rather, the medical staff derives its authority from the governing body of the hospital, is organized and functions in accordance with bylaws and rules and regulations approved by the governing body, and is accountable to the governing body for its actions.

A different view is that the medical staff is a separate entity within the hospital. This view considers the medical staff to be an unincorporated association of individual physicians holding staff privileges at a particular hospital.

Proponents of this view base their contention on the JCAHO standards that require that the medical staff be a self-governing organization. Additionally, they note that Medicare and Medicaid regulations and state statutes specify that medical staffs must be separately organized. On the basis of these considerations, it is argued that medical staffs represent entities separate from hospitals.

The law in this area is unsettled. Court decisions can be cited that appear to support both viewpoints. However, both JCAHO standards and state statutes place the ultimate authority and responsibility for hospital activities with the hospital's governing body. To consider the medical staff an independent legal entity would appear to be inconsistent with these standards and statutes. Additionally, it would undercut the authority and responsibility of the hospital's governing body for the care provided by and within the hospital. Finally, medical staffs that act as entities independent of the hospital risk incurring liability under antitrust, tax, tort, and Medicare-Medicaid antifraud and abuse law that they would otherwise not incur.

The organization of a medical staff is accomplished in accordance with the medical staff's bylaws. The JCAHO requires that "the medical staff develops and adopts bylaws and rules and regulations to establish a framework for self-governance of medical staff activities and accountability to the governing body."[2] The JCAHO further specifies that the medical staff bylaws should include provisions for:

- An executive committee that is empowered to act on behalf of the medical staff between meetings.
- Fair hearing and appellate review mechanisms.
- Mechanisms for corrective action.
- A description of the organization of the medical staff, including categories of staff membership.
- Requirements for frequency of meetings and for attendance.
- A mechanism for ensuring effective communication among medical staff members.
- A mechanism for amending the bylaws and rules and regulations.
- Participation by the medical staff in any hospital deliberations affecting the discharge of medical staff responsibilities.

In addition, the bylaws must:

- Establish criteria and procedures for appointing new applicants to the medical staff and for reappointing existing members.

- Describe a process for delineating clinical privileges for new members and reappraising clinical privileges of existing members.

- Provide mechanisms for monitoring and evaluating the quality and appropriateness of patient care and the clinical performance of all individuals with clinical privileges.

The medical staff bylaws form a critical document for the organization of the medical staff and for the conduct of its activities. The precise manner by which each medical staff organizes itself and conducts its affairs is left to its discretion and varies widely.

The Function of Medical Staffs

As an organization, the medical staff has two responsibilities for which it is accountable to the hospital's governing body:

- Review of the ethical conduct and professional practices of its members.

- Monitoring the quality of all medical care provided to patients.

To fulfill these responsibilities, the medical staff is expected, in accordance with its bylaws, to:

- Review and make recommendations regarding medical staff membership and the exercise of clinical privileges.

- Recommend corrective actions that may result in the restriction or termination of clinical privileges.

- Monitor the performance of members of the medical staff.

In accordance with the requirements of the JCAHO, monitoring and evaluation of the quality and appropriateness of patient care and the clinical performance of all individuals with clinical privileges is accomplished through:

- Monthly meetings of clinical departments or major clinical services.

- Surgical case review.

- Drug usage evaluation.

- Review of medical records.

- Review of blood usage.

- Monitoring pharmacy and therapeutics function.

The JCAHO's *Accreditation Manual for Hospitals* provides more detailed descriptions of the characteristics that pertain to each of these activities.[3] In addition, the JCAHO specifies that the medical staff is expected to participate in other hospitalwide review functions, including infection control, internal and external disaster plans, hospital safety, and utilization review.

In order to ensure that quality assurance activities result in improved patient care, several methods have been proposed for incorporating the results of the various review activities into the reappointment and recredentialing processes.[4-6] Implementation of these proposals offers the hope that the considerable time and effort expended by medical staffs on quality assurance activities will lead to enhanced clinical performance and improved patient care. More on this may be found in Chapters Three and Five of this monograph.

References

1. *Accreditation Manual for Hospitals*. Chicago, Ill.: Joint Commission on Accreditation of Healthcare Organizations, 1989, MS.1, p. 101.

2. *Ibid*, MS.2, p. 104.

3. *Ibid*, MS.6, p. 117-122.

4. Horwitz, M. "Measuring Quality of Care." *Medical Staff Counselor* 1(1):31-8, Winter 1988.

5. Thompson, R. "Exploding 12 Myths about Quality Assurance and Peer Review." *Medical Staff Counselor* 1(2):39,50, Spring 1988.

6. Cowan, D. "Reappointment and Recredentialing." *Medical Staff Management* 1(11):3-4, Nov. 1988, and 1(12):4-5, Dec. 1988.

Dale H. Cowan, MD, JD, is Director, Hematology and Oncology, Marymount Hospital, Garfield Heights, Ohio. He is Chair of the College's Forum on Law and Medicine.

Chapter Three

Guidelines for Medical Quality Management Program Development

by Edward H. Lipson, MD, MS, FACPE

Authority and Responsibility

The hospital governing body has the ultimate authority and responsibility for monitoring the quality of care provided in the hospital.[1] Most hospital governing bodies delegate the responsibility for implementation of a medical quality management program (MQMP) to the organized medical staff. Day-to-day program development and implementation are a collaborative effort of the hospital's management team and medical staff leadership. In many hospitals, the medical director or vice president for medical affairs is the key management representative charged with working with the medical staff on MQMP development.[2]

The MQMP can be structured in various forms, but the functions that these programs must undertake are well defined by the Joint Commission on Accreditation of Healthcare Organizations (JCAHO)[3] and by statute in many states.[4] From a practical standpoint, meeting JCAHO standards and receiving JCAHO accreditation is mandatory for most hospitals, because the Medicare program requires that hospitals be JCAHO-accredited to receive Medicare reimbursement (see Chapter 1). The medical staff bylaws outline the committee structure that a particular medical staff employs to carry out its delegated responsibilities for implementing the MQMP.

MQMP Monitoring Functions

The scope of the medical staff functions that the MQMP must perform includes:[5]

- Monitoring and evaluation of the quality and appropriateness of patient care provided by all individuals with clinical privileges.

- Surgical case review.

- Drug usage evaluation.

- Medical record review.
- Blood usage review.
- Pharmacy and therapeutics function.

The medical staff must also participate in other hospital review functions, including risk management activities, infection control, internal and external disaster plans, hospital safety, and utilization review.

In addition to the required medical staff functions, the MQMP must provide for monitoring and evaluation of the quality and appropriateness of patient care in the following services:

- Alcoholism and other drug dependence services, when provided.
- Diagnostic radiology services.
- Dietetic services.
- Emergency services.
- Hospital-sponsored ambulatory care services.
- Nuclear medicine services.
- Nursing services.
- Pathology and medical laboratory services.
- Pharmaceutical services.
- Physician rehabilitation services.
- Radiation oncology services.
- Respiratory care services.
- Social work services.
- Special care units.
- Surgical and anesthesia services.

Monitoring and evaluation of the care provided in these services does not fall solely to the medical staff, but physicians will naturally be heavily involved in many of these functions of the hospitalwide MQMP. Frequently, departments such as radiology or respiratory care will have physician directors who are responsible for implementing a department-specific MQMP.

Implementation of the various medical staff and departmental functions that must be accomplished by the MQMP requires a process that is comprehensive, coordinated, and efficient. Various systems have been proposed for this process, of which the Medical Management Analysis (MMA) system of Joyce Craddick, MD, is a prominent example.[6] The building blocks of MMA are:

- Monitoring and problem identification.
- Assessment of problems.
- Follow-up action, problem resolution, and documentation.

The essence of Dr. Craddick's system is the screening of every patient record to identify adverse patient occurrences (occurrence screening) using various outcome criteria. The MQMP functions outlined above serve as data sources for the occurrence screening process.

The JCAHO, as part of its Agenda for Change,[7] is undertaking a major redirection of its accreditation program. This initiative emphasizes the need to assess an organization's ability to provide high-quality care and whether this goal is actually achieved.

The hospital's ability to provide high-quality care is embodied in the structure and process variables of quality, while reaching this goal represents the outcome variable.[8] The MQMP may be viewed as a part of the hospital's self-regulatory apparatus that constitutes a structural component of quality. In the past, the JCAHO's accreditation process has been oriented primarily toward assessing the structure variable, with some attempt to assess the process variable of quality. The Agenda for Change places greater emphasis on assessment of the outcome of patient care.

To better address clinical outcomes, the JCAHO is developing a comprehensive screening process that uses critical clinical indicators and threshold criteria. This screening process shares many of the features of MMA and other occurrence screening methods. It envisions an ongoing screening and evaluation of information about important aspects of patient care and also identifies opportunities for improving care. The JCAHO does not seek to independently judge quality but rather to evaluate the effectiveness of various hospital activities, including MQMP, in ensuring the provision of high-quality care.[9]

MQMP Structure

The organizational structure that is developed to carry out the MQMP should flow logically from the required review functions and from comprehensive screening process activities. Many of the functions described above customarily are carried out by a medical staff committee that is delineated in the medical staff bylaws. Because of the large number of required monitoring functions, this presents an organizational challenge for efficiency. Indeed, many physicians view committees with suspicion and are reluctant to participate because of the demands on their time. There is also the challenge to make sure that information that is generated by the MQMP flows to the right point in the system so that it can be acted upon to improve patient care.

There are many differ ways to formulate a medical staff committee structure to meet the needs of the MQMP, but most formulations share certain key features:

- Reporting of results to the governing body.

Because the governing body has the ultimate authority and responsibility for the quality of care in the hospital, there should be a mechanism for keeping the governing body apprised of the activities of the MQMP on a regular basis.[10] This can be accomplished through a joint conference committee comprising representatives from the medical staff, the governing body, and administration; a subcommittee of the governing body, such as a professional affairs committee; or a report to the governing body at its regularly scheduled meeting by the chief of staff, the medical director, or another appropriate physician leader.

- Medical Staff Executive Committee.

The medical staff executive committee is required by the JCAHO,[11] is the primary "action" committee of the medical staff,[12] and is responsible to the governing body for implementing the MQMP.

- Departmental Committees.

In most hospitals, departments representing the main clinical services support the executive committee in carrying out its delegated responsibilities. The departments monitor care within their clinical purview and report the results to the executive committee. In small hospitals, the executive committee takes direct responsibility for monitoring care across clinical services.

- Review Function Committees.

The required review functions described previously are often carried out by separate committees to ensure proper focus and attention to essential review activities. These committees include:

Surgical Case Review--In the past, this committee was usually called the tissue committee. The need to review surgical cases in which tissue is not removed, however, means that the scope of the tissue committee must be expanded to include review of all surgical cases. Many medical staffs do not have a separate surgical case review committee. Instead, they report the results of this monitoring function directly to the appropriate departmental committee.

Medical Records--This committee should meet at least quarterly to review the quality of medical records for clinical pertinence and timely completion. Some medical staffs have chosen to have this function reported directly to the appropriate departmental committee rather than designating a separate committee.

Blood Usage--Also known as the transfusion committee, this committee evaluates the appropriateness of use of blood products and monitors transfusion reactions.

Pharmacy and Therapeutics--This committee handles the required review function pertaining to development and maintenance of the hospital's drug formulary; review of untoward drug reactions; and evaluation of investigational or experimental drugs. The drug usage evaluation function is also frequently handled by this committee. Failure to effectively carry out a monitoring program of drug usage is one of the most frequent shortcomings cited by the JCAHO.[13]

- Other Review Activities.

As noted previously, the medical staff must also participate in other hospital review functions, including risk management activities, infection control, internal and external disaster plans, hospital safety and utilization review. Many medical staffs develop separate committees to deal with these issues. The risk management function, in particular, has received special attention from the JCAHO in its most recent accreditation guidelines.[14] It is essential that information on adverse patient occurrences flow into the MQMP for analysis and appropriate action by the medical staff.

The other required review activities listed above do not fall primarily to the medical staff, but they may require medical staff input. These activities may be overseen by hospital committees on which physicians are represented.

- MQMP Committee.

Many medical staffs have found it helpful to have the various review committees and functions report to a coordinating and oversight committee. This committee, sometimes termed the quality assurance committee, receives reports from the review functions and directs the flow of information to the appropriate location for action, such as a departmental committee, a hospital department, another medical staff committee, or the executive committee. Some medical staffs have found it helpful to underscore the important role of this committee by designating the vice chief of staff as the MQMP committee chairman. The activities of this committee are reported to the executive committee.

- MQMP Department.

The hospital medical staff does not have the financial or human resources to develop and implement a comprehensive MQMP. It falls to hospital management to supply professional and support staff to help carry out the required review functions. This department has the responsibility for data collection and support of the medical staff review committees. It also serves as the coordination point between the hospital committees and the medical staff committees. It is the key integration point for hospitalwide MQMP activities.

In Dr. Joyce Craddick's MMA system, this department performs or coordinates the hospitalwide activities of problem identification, referral of problems for assessment and follow-up action, and monitoring of follow-up actions.[15]

It is again important to note that physician time devoted to the MQMP is a precious resource that must be used wisely. A well-operated MQMP department can ensure efficient use of physician time and thereby obtain the critical "buy-in" and support of the medical staff.

Summary: Key Issues for Program Performance

- Information Flow.

A key element of the MQMP is information flow. Too often, review and monitoring activities occur in isolation, and crucial information for improving patient care never gets to the right point in the system. The MQMP department and committee play key roles in ensuring smooth information flow.

Two of the most critical information pathways are from the risk management function to the MQMP and from the MQMP to the credentialing function. As discussed in Chapter 4 of this monograph, it is essential that each member of the medical staff undergo a periodic performance reappraisal.[16] The data for the reappraisal process must be supplied by the MQMP. The goal is to have objective data on individual performance available for use as part of the reappointment decision.

- Information Use.

Data collected as part of the MQMP must be analyzed and evaluated by individuals who are in positions to make informed judgments. Nothing is served by having data entered into a "black hole." The critical locus for information use is the clinical department, usually defined as the active staff of that department. Information from the MQMP must be shared with the active staff so that corrective action can be taken as necessary and the results monitored.

Key Role for the Physician Executive: A Model

As noted previously, the physician executive (medical director, vice-president for medical affairs, etc.) can play a key role in ensuring successful development of MQMP with the requisite functional and structural attributes. One model is to place the physician executive in a position of authority and responsibility for the MQMP. In this model, the following departments/functions would have a direct reporting relationship to the physician executive:

- Medical Staff Office (credentialing, reappraisal, and reappointment of the medical staff).
- Utilization Review.
- Medical Quality Management (quality assurance).
- Medical Records.
- Infection Control.
- Risk Management.

The physician executive in this model reports to the chief executive officer or chief of operations, with liaison responsibilities to the chief of staff.

This model helps ensure the necessary integration of the various MQMP functions, facilitates essential input from the medical staff, provides support for the chief of staff in carrying out the medical staff's board-delegated responsibilities for the MQMP, and creates a knowledgeable advocate for high-quality patient care on the hospital's management team. In this role, the physician executive can act as the driving force behind the hospital's efforts to constantly improve the quality of care.

References

1. Joint Commission on Accreditation of Healthcare Organizations. *Accreditation Manual for Hospitals*. Chicago: JCAHO, 1989, Standard QA.1.1., p. 219.

2. Couch, J. *Medical Quality Management for Physician Executives in the 1990s: The Essentials of Medical Quality Management*. Tampa, Fla.: American College of Physician Executives, 1988, p. 24.

3. JCAHO. *op. cit.*, pp. 219-23.

4. See, for example, the *California Business and Professions Code*, Chapter 5, Article 12, Section 2282.

5. JCAHO. *op. cit.*, pp. 117-122, 220.

6. Craddick, J. *Medical Management Analysis: A Systematic Approach to Quality Assurance and Risk Management*, Volume 1. Auburn, Calif.: Joyce W. Craddick, MD, 1983

7. Couch, J. *Medical Quality Management for Physician Executives in the 1990s: Preparing for the Joint Commission's New Initiatives*. Tampa, Fla.: American College of Physician Executives, 1988, pp. 17-22.

8. Donabedian, A. *Explorations in Quality Assessment and Monitoring: The Definition of Quality and Approaches to Its Assessment*, Volume 1. Ann Arbor, Mich.: Health Administration Press, 1980.

9. Couch, J. *Medical Quality Management for Physician Executives in the 1990s: Preparing for the Joint Commission's New Initiatives*. Tampa, Fla.: American College of Physician Executives, 1988, pp. 18.

10. JCAHO. *op. cit.*, Standard QA1.2., p. 219.

11. Ibid, pp. 101-123.

12. Eisele, C., and others *The Medical Staff and the Modern Hospital*. Englewood, Colo.: Estes Park Institute, 1985, p. 23.

13. California Medical Association, review of 125 consecutive survey reports, 1987.

14. JCAHO. *op. cit.*, p. 219, QA1.4 and QA1.5.

15. Craddick, *op. cit.*, p. 50.

16. JCAHO. *op. cit.*, p. 221, Standard QA2.5.1.

Edward H. Lipson, MD, MS, FACPE, is Director of Physician Consulting Services for National Medical Audit, San Francisco, Calif. He is a member of the College's Forum on Quality Health Care.

Chapter Four

Legal Aspects of Physician Credentialing

by Todd Sagin, MD, JD

Erosion of Charitable Immunity

American hospitals have always competed for highly respected physicians to join their medical staffs. For most physicians, securing privileges at a local hospital is essential to the practice of medicine. However, it is only relatively recently that hospitals have had to worry about liability for insufficiently screening medical staff applicants or monitoring current staff to ensure the practice of high-caliber medicine. Courts have determined that legal ramifications arise out of the procedures by which hospital privileges and memberships are granted, restricted, or denied.

Early in the evolution of U.S. hospital law, hospitals were regarded as charitable health care institutions and were protected by a doctrine of charitable immunity. This common law doctrine, in effect in some jurisdictions until the 1940s, declared hospitals to be benefactors that could not be sued by patient beneficiaries even for the most obvious negligence of their employees. Even in jurisdictions where the charitable immunity shield began to disintegrate, physicians and nurses were, from the courts' perspective, "independent contractors" even when directly employed by the health care facility. It was contended that hospitals could not exercise effective supervision and control over the professional component of the services delivered by these "independent contractors."

This perspective began to change after World War II as hospitals became more complex institutions. Courts began to realize not only that hospitals were in a position to influence their professional employees, but also that it was easier for health care institutions to absorb the risks of loss posed by negligent medical practice than for individual patients or even physicians to do so. Furthermore, insurance became readily available to protect the assets of institutions. Courts therefore began to apply to hospitals the concept of *respondeat superior* traditionally applied to other corporate entities. This is basically a concept of vicarious liability where the employer is automatically liable for the negligence of its employees. The leading case reflecting this change in perspective is *Bing v. Thunig* 2 N.Y. 2nd 656, 143 N.E. 2nd 3 (1957), wherein the court noted that "the conception that the hospital does not undertake to treat the patient, does not undertake to act through its doctors and nurses, but undertakes instead simply to procure them to act upon their own responsibility, no longer reflects fact."

Liability For Independent Contractors

As a general rule, however, hospitals were still not held liable for the acts of their nonemployed attending physicians, because these doctors, rather than the hospital, maintain the primary relationship with the patient and are presumed to act autonomously. However, there are two major exceptions to this principle expressed in modern case law. The first is where a physician, although technically an independent contractor, is acting on behalf of the health care institution and therefore is deemed a de facto employee. The second exception, which will be explored more fully in the remainder of this chapter, holds a hospital responsible when it fails to adequately review the credentials of applicants to its medical staff or insufficiently monitors the performance of its attending staff. This responsibility attaches to the hospital under the doctrine of corporate negligence or corporate liability. It makes the hospital the primary instrumentality in the monitoring of the quality of health care delivered by its staff. This responsibility, deviation from which is a form of active negligence, is reinforced by state and federal licensing regulations, by JCAHO and other accreditation standards, and frequently by local health code requirements.

Corporate Liability

As discussed in Chapters 1 and 2 of this monograph, case law has supported the conclusion that the hospital medical staff is an integral component of the hospital corporation and therefore shares credentialing and monitoring responsibility with the hospital's administration and board of trustees. Although one of the first cases establishing corporate liability for hospitals, *Darling v. Charleston Community Memorial Hospital* 33 Ill. 2d 236, 211 N.E. 2d 253 (1965), was decided in 1965, it was not until the unfavorable malpractice climate of the 1970s that cases holding facilities responsible for negligently credentialing and monitoring attending physicians became frequent. In *Gonzales v. Nork* No. 228 566 (Cal. Super Ct., Sacramento Co.)(1974), the court noted that "all powers of the medical staff flow from the board of trustees, and the staff must be held accountable for its control of quality. If the quality is not controlled, the hospital may be subjected to corporate liability. The medical staff acts for the hospital in the discharge of the hospital's responsibilities to protect its patients." Numerous other cases have adopted and reinforced this stance --e.g., *Elam v. College Park Hospital* 4 Civ. No. 24479 (Cal. Ct. App.)(1982); *Corleto v. Shore Memorial*

Hospital 138 N.J. Super 203, 350 A 2nd 534 (1975); and *Johnson v. Misericodia Hospital*, 99 Wisc 2d 708, 301 N.W.2d 156 (1981).

The responsibility of the medical staff for monitoring the quality of medical care compels it to review appointments, monitor the ethical and professional practices of its staff, and consider the termination or restriction of privileges where appropriate. Detailed credentialing procedures are outlined in some state statutes or hospital codes and in JCAHO accreditation manuals. Participation in some federal health care programs, for example Medicare, also requires that the hospital meet specifications regarding peer review of physician competence.

Physician Rights

It is clear that a hospital has a legal obligation to go to considerable lengths to ensure the competence of physicians practicing under its auspices. However, in doing so, the hospital may not disregard the rights of physicians. The authority to practice medicine is not an inalienable right but rather a privilege granted by society to members who meet select criteria. Likewise, there is no constitutional right to staff privileges at a medical institution, even if the access to resources afforded by such privileges is essential to the practice of modern medicine--*Hayman v. Galveston* 273 U.S 414 (1927). Courts have been inclined, however, to recognize membership on the hospital staff as valuable property interest that may be protected under some circumstances--*Chrisihil v. Annapolis Emergency Hospital Association, Inc.* 496 F.2d 174 (4th Cir. 1974), vacated & remanded on damages only, 522 F.2d 1070 (1977).

When physicians challenge denials or restrictions of medical staff privileges, they frequently seek redress in court contending one or all of three general categories of injury by the defendant hospital:

- Failure to provide fundamental fairness (due process) in the peer review undertaking.
- Failure to follow hospital by-laws.
- Restraint of trade.

The first of these complaints, failure to provide for fundamental fairness in the credentialing process, is based on the due process clauses of the Fifth and Fourteenth Amendments to the U.S. Constitution. All public or government health facilities are compelled by these due process clauses to provide a number of procedural safeguards when acting on medical staff privilege requests. The Fourteenth Amendment also provides for equal protection of the laws, thereby prohibiting hospitals from denying or restricting staff privileges based on racial discrimination or discrimination based on another prohibited or arbitrary criterion. These constitutional restrictions apply clearly only to public hospitals, because it is "state action" that is limited by these constitutional amendments. As a result, there has been considerable litigation trying to determine whether tax-exempt hospitals receiving government funds can be characterized such that they fall under the constitutional "state action" proscriptions. If a hospital was determined to be private, courts routinely have found their decisions concerning medical staff not to be subject to judicial review.

In recent years, other legal requirements, applicable to both private and public hospitals, have made reliance on constitutional requirements less necessary and the distinction between private and public hospitals largely moot when dealing with credentialing and privileging issues. The courts, recognizing that important public and private rights are at stake in the medical staff appointment process, have over the past two decades steadily whittled away at the autonomy they previously granted the governing boards of private hospitals. An early example is *Greisman v. Newcomb Hospital* 40 N.J. 389, 192 A2d 817 (1963), in which the court announced that the hospital decision to deny an osteopath staff privileges was subject to judicial review, not because of constitutional requirements but rather to ensure that the hospital was exercising its powers reasonably and on behalf of the public welfare. The court premised its right to carry out such judicial review on common law principles of fairness and on public policy considerations. Other courts have declared hospitals "quasi-public" because of their critical function in the community. Courts in numerous states have now held that private hospital decisions will be reviewed to ensure that medical staff decisions are not capricious, arbitrary, or unreasonable--*Ascherman v. San Francisco Medical Society* 39 Cal. App. 2d 623, 114 Cal. Rpts. 631 (1974); *Woodward v. Porter Hospital, Inc.* 125 Vt. 419, 217 A.2d 37 (1966); *Garrow v. Elizabeth General Hospital and Dispensary* 79 N.J. 549, 401 A2d 533 (1979); and *Bricker v. Sceva Speare Memorial Hospital* 287 A2d 589 (1971).

When complying with due process requirements, it is helpful to be cognizant of the two distinct theories of law that constitute this concept. The first is procedural mechanisms that ensure a fair and thorough consideration of the issues involved. The second, substantive due process, requires that the criteria by which staff applicants are judged not be capricious or arbitrary. These criteria should have some reasonable relationship to the goals and mission of the hospital (e.g. delivery of high-quality care). Increasingly, courts have allowed hospitals to develop criteria specific to their institutional needs. The following are generally acceptable criteria for consideration in granting or renewing staff privileges:

- A completed application that contains no false or misleading information.
- Adequate education, training, and experience, including residency completion and board certification.
- Ability to work with others.
- Ability to provide peer recommendations.
- Need in the hospital for the applicant's particular skills.
- No overtaxing of the hospital's resources or facilities.
- Maintenance of adequate liability insurance.
- Commitment to the hospital as the physician's primary inpatient facility.
- Willingness to comply with hospital by-laws and policies.
- Maintenance of demonstrable level of clinical competence.
- Demonstration of continuing good moral character and ethical practice.
- Complete, accurate, and timely recordkeeping.
- Absence of conflicts of interest.
- Adequate physical and mental health.
- Adequate proximity to the hospital.
- A history of disciplinary actions by licensing authorities.
- Restriction or removal of privileges at another health care facility.

This list is by no means complete, but it gives examples of criteria that can be reasonably related to the average hospital's goals and mission. Where special circumstances exist, additional criteria may be warranted. For example, hospitals with medical school affiliations may require their physicians to obtain faculty appointments as a condition of staff membership--*Dillard v. Rowland* 520 S.W. 2d 81 (Mo. App. 1974). The hospital should be able to demonstrate that this requirement is based on its desire to enhance the quality of its staff and that the faculty appointment process itself is based on legitimate criteria, such as the ability to supervise students.

Courts have granted hospitals considerable discretion in elaborating staff credentialing and privileging criteria, as long as the standards themselves or their application are not arbitrary, capricious, or unreasonable. Physicians challenging such criteria often complain that the standards by which they are being judged lack specificity. However courts have allowed considerable generality to prevail in the establishment of credentialing standards. For example, acceptable to a Florida court were bylaws allowing a physician to be suspended for failing to "conform to the accepted standard of practice for treatment of patients in this district"--*North Broward Hospital District v. Mizell* 148 So. 2d 1,5 (Fla. 1962).

Challenges to some credentialing standards have had success in court. It is now widely accepted that discrimination based on schools of practice (that is, allopathic versus osteopathic) is not a valid basis for denying staff membership. In some jurisdictions, this proscription is bolstered by state statutes as well--for example, Florida Statute 395.011 (1) and (4). The classic case for this finding of a per se illegal boycott was *Weiss v. York Hospital* 745 F.2d 786 (3d Cir. 1984). Discrimination based on race, creed, sex, color, age, or national origin is prohibited by an array of federal and state constitutional provisions and statutes. Discriminating against physicians who choose to participate in alternative health delivery and insurance arrangements may also be disallowed by courts. Courts have also disallowed the requirement that an applicant to the staff be a member of the local medical society--*Foster v. Mobile County Hospital Board* 398 F.2d 227 (5th Cir. 1968). Finally, it has been deemed inappropriate to require that new physician applicants be sponsored by a current member of the medical staff. Such a requirement would allow current staff to apply discriminatory or arbitrary reasons in keeping a physician off the staff.

The mechanics of applying credentialing criteria must comply with constitutional expectations of fairness. Fairness requires that rules be consistently applied and demands that decisions be based on evidence that supports the determination. Although hospitals are not required to implement the elaborate due process requirements of the judicial system, court rulings have made clear those procedures necessary at peer review hearings to ensure the fundamental rights of the parties involved. Development of fair procedures in the credentialing process is also encouraged by JCAHO accreditation requirements, by Medicare's Conditions of Participation, and by the Health Care Quality Improvement Act of 1986 (see Chapter One). Because there has historically been considerable litigation over due process denials, most hospital bylaws have been written to meet these basic requirements.

Physicians facing denials or restrictions of staff privileges are entitled to a hearing before the peer review body making the adverse determination. The hearing must be convened before permanent denial or curtailment of privileges actually takes place. In order to protect the public welfare, most hospital bylaws allow for emergency, temporary suspension of privileges where circumstances warrant--*Citta v. Delaware Valley Hospital* 313 F.

Supp. 301 (E.D. PA.1970). Such summary suspensions should be carried out as soon as the hospital becomes aware of the conduct in question and should be limited to circumstances in which the physician's continued presence on the staff creates a serious patient care problem--*Park Hospital District v. District Court* 555 P.2d 984 (Cal. Sup. Ct. 1976).

Physicians must also be given timely and adequate notice of the hearing in a manner that makes clear the charges against them--*Silver v. Castle Memorial Hospital* 53 Hawaii 475, 497 P.2d 564 (1972). Adequate notice is an amount of time reasonable for the physician to prepare a defense. Physicians facing rejection of an initial medical staff application, denial of reappointment, or curtailment of privileges should be given a written statement specifying the reasons for the action.

In general, unless the hospital requests legal representation to be present, the physician is not entitled to representation by counsel during a hearing. This is to protect the peer review character of the hearing, which is not meant to be adversarial. New Jersey, however, has recognized a role for an attorney in such hearings to assist in advising his client, presenting evidence, challenging or explaining adverse evidence, and presenting arguments. Furthermore, the Health Care Quality Improvement Act of 1986, a piece of federal legislation addressed more fully in Chapter One, suggests detailed procedural guidelines for peer review that include representation by an attorney. This is not a mandatory guideline, but many hospitals are likely to comply with the Act's recommendation by altering their bylaws to afford a right to counsel.

To provide a defense to an adverse determination, the physician must have access to the documents examined by those making the unfavorable ruling--*Chrisihil v. Annapolis Emergency Hospital Association, Inc.* 496 F.2d 174 (4th Cir. 1974). Although typically this means access to patient charts, under some circumstances it may include confidential peer review statements in the physician's file. In *Garrow v. Elizabeth General Hospital and Dispensary* 79 N.J. 549, 401 A2d 533 (1979), a New Jersey court allowed release of such a file to a physician challenging his denial of medical staff membership. The court believed that due process required that the physician have access to that material upon which the hospital's board of trustees had relied when rejecting his staff application. The court did not require the hospital to disclose the source of information in the file unless it was particularly critical to preparation of the defense. In general, however, courts are inclined to protect the confidentiality of peer review documents in order to promote the public policy goals of peer review. Hospitals have persuasively argued that disclosure of such information would seriously damage their efforts to obtain information critical to the peer review/quality assurance process. Furthermore, several states have enacted statutes that provide for the confidentiality of statements gathered by peer review committees.[1]

In carrying out peer review, an objective and impartial panel of physicians is a basic condition of procedural due process. Courts generally presume the fair-mindedness of such a hearing panel, and anyone challenging this supposition must bear the burden of proving impartiality or bias affecting the decision-making process. In *Klinge v. Lutheran Charities Association of St. Louis* 523 F.2d 56 (8th Cir. 1975), the court noted "...plaintiff was not entitled to a panel made up of outsiders or doctors who had never heard of the case and who knew nothing about the facts of it or what they supposed the facts to be." Nevertheless, many institutions are likely to change their bylaws in order to come under the immunity protections of the Health Care Quality Improvement Act mentioned previously. This Act suggests that hearings be conducted before one of the following:

- An arbitrator agreed to mutually by the health care institution and the physician involved.
- A panel of individual physicians, appointed by the hospital, who are not in direct economic competition with the physician being reviewed.
- A hearing officer, appointed by the hospital, who is not in economic competition with the physician under review.

The hearing itself must be conducted in a manner that allows the physician to call and confront witnesses, present evidence in his or her defense, and record or transcribe all the statements made at the hearing. The panel weighing the evidence must base its decision on substantial evidence produced at the hearing and cannot rely on communications made to it outside the proceedings. Decisions by the panel should be rendered in writing, with an explanation of the basis for the determination. Initial applicants for staff membership are generally expected to bear the burden of proof for demonstrating they meet the institution's requirements for clinical privileges. For physicians who are already on the medical staff, it is the hospital that usually must show why the doctor should have his privileges removed or restricted. Health care institutions are expected to base their determinations on substantial evidence. For physicians challenging the findings of the health care facility, a higher level of proof is frequently required. In order to prevail, such physicians may have to produce "clear and convincing" evidence that the hospital's judgment was ill founded. Final decisions in any significant disciplinary matter lie with the hospital's governing body.

Review of the matter by the governing body should be limited to the record of the hearing panel. A new hearing before the governing body is not required and in general new evidence should not be introduced at this stage of review and appeal. The hospital governing body may accept the determination of the medical staff hearing panel or send the issue back to it for further consideration. JCAHO suggests that such further consideration regarding appointment or privileges be carried out by a panel composed jointly of medical staff and hospital board members. Ultimate authority, however, remains with the governing body regarding any appointment or privileges recommendations.

Physicians may challenge credentialing or privileging determinations on grounds other than due process. When hospitals fail to comply with their own bylaws, liability may ensue (see Chapter Two of this monograph). Exactly when and to what extent bylaws must be followed has generated some litigation in recent years.

The hospital's deviation from procedures outlined in its bylaws must be significant before liability can be imposed. That is, the deviation must in some way prejudice the rights of the physician claiming injury. Furthermore, the physician must object to such substantive procedural defects in a timely manner or his right to contest the irregularity may be waived--*Kennedy v. St. Joseph Memorial Hospital of Kokoma Indiana, Inc*. 482 N.E. 2d 268 (Ind. Ct. App. 1985). The advice of legal counsel can be extremely helpful when exploring potential liability for procedural defects.

Where a hospital unilaterally adopts changes in bylaws, physicians may claim unfair and arbitrary deprivation of the protections and rights formerly found in the bylaws. The law in this area is not entirely settled at this time, and legal counsel should be sought when conflicts arise around such change.

Clinical Performance Profiling

The pressures of cost containment in the health care field are generating new potential challenges to physician access to staff membership and clinical privileges. Health care institutions have a compelling need in today's competitive environment to have a medical staff that practices high-quality medicine in a cost-effective manner. Where physician behavior threatens the financial health of the institution, a hospital's ability to achieve its goals and mission are threatened. We can therefore expect to see new staff membership criteria emerging that look at a physician's clinical performance from the perspective of cost-effectiveness. The installation of elaborate data monitoring systems in many hospitals allows these institutions to establish economic profiles of specific physicians. Similar profiles may be available from insurance companies, managed care programs, or state health data commissions.

Courts have upheld the right of a hospital to impose requirements designed to protect its financial resources in cases where physicians have been required to carry malpractice insurance--*Holmes v. Hoemako Hospital* 117 Ariz. 403, 573 P.2d 477 (1977). It is likely that future rulings will support a hospital's restriction on medical staff privileges when reasonably related to the institution's need for financial stability.

Antitrust Issues

The efforts of hospitals to comply rigorously with due process requirements for staff credentialing and privileging have forced physicians facing exclusions or restrictions to look to antitrust laws for relief. The denial of staff privileges has accounted for the greatest number of antitrust suits involving hospitals. Alleging antitrust violations, physicians can sue both hospitals and health care practitioners involved in staff privilege determination, charging the peer review process with restraint of competition because it empowers other physicians to determine who will practice in potential competition with themselves. Suit under federal antitrust law has additional appeal because it allows for treble damages and recovery of costs and attorney's fees for successful plaintiffs.

Historically, the activities of professionals were considered exempt from antitrust scrutiny, as were activities that did not have a substantial impact on interstate commerce. However, in recent years, this immunity for professionals has been eliminated, and courts have no longer been willing to show deference to the health care industry when applying antitrust principles. They have also found that hospitals engage in interstate commerce when they treat out-of-state patients or buy supplies from companies located in other states.

Anticompetitive conduct under the law is of two types: that which is per se unlawful and that which is unlawful under a "rule of reason" standard. Under a "per se unlawful" standard, simply establishing that the conduct in question actually took place is adequate to establish antitrust liability. Such conduct is considered so egregious that further examination of the circumstances is not necessary. A potential per se activity of relevance to this discussion on credentialing is the group boycott or concerted refusal to deal.

The "rule of reason" standard requires a weighing and balancing of the procompetitive and anticompetitive effects of the challenged action within the relevant market. Litigation under this standard allows defendants greater opportunity to explain the motivations and effects of their actions. As a general rule, the denial of staff privileges is subject to a rule of reason analysis.

Most physician-related antitrust litigation has come in the area of "group boycotts," usually arising in the context of denied staff privileges. To be illegal, such a group boycott must involve a conspiracy, a refusal to deal or a boycott, a purpose, and an effect of freezing out a competitor. The litigated cases tend to focus on whether or not a conspiracy existed and whether the purpose of denying a physician's application for privileges was motivated by economic reasons. Typically, one of four conspiratorial combinations is alleged:

- The medical staff and the hospital.
- The individual members of the staff conspiring among themselves.
- Individual staff members conspiring with the hospital.
- The hospital entering into an exclusive contract with a physician or group.

To establish concerted action, a plaintiff must establish "a conscious commitment to a common scheme designed to achieve an unlawful objective." Where a hospital has not established clear, independent reasons for denying staff privileges, it may be found guilty of conspiring with competing physicians who have recommended denial of staff privileges.

Exclusive agreements are not infrequently arranged between hospitals and providers in departments such a radiology, anesthesiology, and pathology. These contracts may give specified physicians the sole right to practice in these specialties, or the hospital may limit privileges in certain areas to the hospital's full-time staff. Such arrangements have been attacked by excluded physicians as group boycotts in violation of antitrust law. Courts have generally found such contracts to serve legitimate hospital needs and therefore to be acceptable--*Dos-Santos v. Columbus-Cuneo-Cabrini Medical Center* 684 F.2d 1346 (7th Cir. 1982).

The most important case in this area under federal law has been the 1984 decision of the United States Supreme Court in *Jefferson Parish Hospital District No. 2 v. Hyde* 104 S. Ct. 1551 (1984). As a result of an exclusive contract between an anesthesiology group and the hospital, Dr. Hyde had been denied hospital privileges. He charged that the hospital illegally tied anesthesiology services to the provision of other medical services, particularly surgery and operating room services. In three separate opinions, the Supreme Court Justices agreed that such exclusive contracts were not automatically illegal but must be analyzed on a case-by-case basis. In *Hyde*, the court determined that there was no shortage of comparable hospitals in the area from which anesthesia or surgical services could be obtained. Therefore, because the hospital did not have market power in providing hospital services, the tying arrangement should be analyzed under a rule of reason standard and was not per se illegal. Under such a standard, it is the plaintiff who must demonstrate that the arrangement unreasonably restrains competition. In the *Hyde* case, the court found the contract legal because there was no evidence that it had adversely affected the price, supply, demand for, or quality of anesthesiology services.

As a result of the ruling in *Hyde*, hospitals considering exclusive contracts with physician groups should make sure to justify the arrangement on grounds of hospital efficiency and patient care. If contracts are properly drafted along those lines, this ruling should make it particularly difficult for future challenges to denial of privileges in the context of exclusive contracts. This is particularly so in urban settings where hospitals are less likely to have market power sufficient to raise antitrust concerns. However, where little competition exists, where only one hospital in an area has specialized facilities, or where all hospitals function under an exclusive contract arrangement for the same particular group's services, antitrust concerns must be explored.

In *Weiss v. York Hospital*, the court considered an antitrust class action brought by an osteopath against a hospital and its medical staff alleging that osteopaths were the targets of an illegal group boycott. The court found that the hospital's medical staff was a combination of individual doctors who were capable of entering into a conspiracy among themselves. The court found that the conduct of the medical staff, which dominated the credentialing process, amounted to a per se illegal group boycott, given the evidence that different (stricter) credentialing standards were applied to the osteopaths. Individual staff members were considered by the court to be independent economic entities conspiring for anticompetitive reasons, rather than to meet quality of care objectives. In addition, the court noted that the hospital could not, as a matter of law, conspire with its own medical staff, because all of the staff's responsibilities were delegations from the hospital board.

The court decision in this field receiving the greatest public attention most recently has been *Patrick v. Burget* 108 S. Ct. 1658 (1988). This case was decided by the U.S. Supreme Court after a lower federal district court found members of a hospital credentialing committee violated the first and second sections of the Sherman Antitrust Act.

The Patrick case unfolded in Astoria, Oregon, where Dr. Patrick was employed at the Astoria Clinic and was a member of Columbia Memorial Hospital's medical staff in 1972. The following year, he declined an invitation to become a partner in the clinic and instead began an independent practice in competition with the surgical practice of the clinic. He continued to serve on the hospital medical staff.

After establishing his independent practice, Dr. Patrick found that physicians associated with the Astoria Clinic consistently refused to make referrals to him, even when they did not have a general surgeon on their own staff. Nor would these physicians consult with him or provide backup coverage for his patients.

In 1981, a clinic physician requested the hospital's medical staff executive committee to institute a review of Dr. Patrick's hospital privileges. This committee then voted to terminate the privileges, alleging substandard patient care on the part of Dr. Patrick. A hearing committee was convened at Dr. Patrick's request to review the charges and to hear Dr. Patrick's defense. This five-member committee was chaired by another Astoria Clinic physician. Rather than risk termination of his privileges, Dr. Patrick resigned from the staff and filed antitrust charges against the physician partners of the Astoria Clinic. A jury awarded damages of $650,000 on the antitrust claims and the court trebled these damages and awarded other expenses, making a total award of nearly $2.3 million. The Ninth Circuit Court of Appeals reversed. This court asserted that, even if the Astoria Clinic physicians had used the peer review process to eliminate a competitor rather than improve patient care, their conduct was immune under a doctrine of state action. This doctrine held that private actions were immune from antitrust scrutiny whenever a state required private health providers to establish peer review and created a licensing procedure to ensure that such peer review could be carried out.

In reversing the Ninth Circuit, the U.S. Supreme Court declared that the anticompetitive conduct must be actively supervised by the state itself in order to fall under the doctrine of state action. The Court commented: "The State does not actively supervise this restraint unless a State official has and exercises ultimate authority over private privilege determinations." In Oregon, the court concluded, this was not the case.

Patrick v. Burget was very much a fact-oriented case. Although many saw it as a setback for stronger peer review immunity, its fallout has yet to be seen. In an interpretation of this ruling by a United States Court of Appeals, the 11th Circuit, in *Bolt v. Halifax Hospital Medical Center* (CA 11, No. 84-3256 (1988), squarely held that judicial review by a state can constitute the requisite "active supervision" enunciated in Patrick. Thus, physician peer reviewers could be afforded more protection from antitrust laws in the future if state courts begin to play an active role in the review of such cases.

However, even if states don't take more active roles either legislatively, administratively, or judicially, as long as physician peer reviewers scrupulously adhere to the substantive and procedural due process safeguards in medical quality management practices intended to improve both the quality and the cost effectiveness of health care delivery cited in this chapter and elsewhere,[2] they should be optimally protected from antitrust and other legal actions by physicians being reviewed under the U.S. Supreme Court's finding in *Patrick v. Burget* and the requirements of the Health Care Quality Improvement Act of 1986. State-of-the-art methods for assessing and improving the quality of medical care are examined from a legal and public policy perspective in Chapter Five.

References

1. Guide to State Peer Review Confidentiality Laws. Chicago, Ill.: *American Medical Association*, 1988.

2. Couch, J. *Medical Quality Management for Physician Executives in the 1990s: The Essentials of Medical Quality Management.* Tampa, Florida: American College of Physician Executives, 1988, Chapter 2.

Todd Sagin, MD, JD, is Associate Director, Family Practice Residency Program, Abington Memorial Hospital, Abington, Pennsylvania. He is a member of the College's Forum on Law and Medicine.

Chapter Five

Legal Aspects of Clinical Outcome Management

by James B. Couch, MD, JD
and Alex R. Rodriguez, MD, FACPE

What Is Clinical Outcome Management

Any effort to define a "new concept" in a discipline runs the risk of oversimplification, on the one hand, and plagiarism, on the other. In a broad sense, clinical outcome management is as old as the healing art itself. The presumptive goal of medical practice has always been to achieve the best possible clinical outcomes for patients. The real question concerns whether the medical care necessary to achieve optimal clinical outcomes is being systematically and scientifically assessed and managed.

Throwing caution to the wind, then, clinical outcome management (at least for the purposes of this chapter) may be defined as **the systematic process of assessing and improving the cost effectiveness of the utilization of those medical care resources necessary to effect an acceptable level of improvement in the health status of individual patients and populations.**

By comparison, medical quality management is somewhat broader, comprising the setting of standards (quality control), the measuring of compliance with those standards (quality assessment), and the taking of systematic steps to meet or exceed those standards (quality improvement or enhancement).[1]

Perhaps the major point of departure of this "definition" of clinical outcome management from others in the health care lexicon is the emphasis on the achievement of what is possible for individual patients and populations within the constraints of available resources. This brings out the fact that health care delivery must be regarded as a service that can only draw upon a certain finite bank of resources.

This country and the world are entering an era in which tight constraints must be imposed in all areas of human endeavor. The ultimate goal of management in any area is to achieve the best possible results with the resources available. In no area is this management discipline more needed, or more deficient, than in health care delivery in this country.[2]

Efficient management of health care resources will continue to evolve within financial management approaches (e.g., prospective pricing, capitated arrangements, and health benefit restructuring) and to become dependent upon systems of *clinical* management. This will be necessary to balance cost restraint with quality improvement in health services. In turn, clinical management systems will increasingly rely upon professional standards of quality of care, data systems required to measure quality, and clinical specialists in outcomes management.[3]

How Might It Work

A practical system of appropriate medical standards, guidelines, and practice criteria that can be used by physicians in caring for their patients--referred to by many physicians as "cookbook medicine"--continues to be devastatingly controversial. Various approaches to outcome management based upon professional practice standards have been providing a bonanza for litigators, a conundrum when patients do not fit the standards, a bureaucrat's paradise, and the last stand for free physicians. To avoid controversy, the developers of standards have clothed their products with euphemistic labels. Congress speaks of "technology assessments"; the National Institutes of Health of "the Consensus Development Program"; the American College of Physicians of the "Clinical Efficacy Assessment Project"; David Eddy, for the Council of Medical Specialty Societies, of "clinical policies"; and the American Medical Association of "DATTA." But those who are devising these aids for physicians are responding to a real problem--the need to sort out and apply more rigorous analysis to the combinations of conflicting, changing, halfway, and unempirical technologies in modern medical practice. The Institute of Medicine's Council on Health Care Technology has identified more than 60 groups engaged in producing assessments.[3]

Most of those involved in assessing medical interventions emphasize the importance of flexibility, branching, and judgment in their application. In situations in which no formal assessments exist, which may describe most medical encounters, outcomes management will need to rely on encounter forms or computerized lists of observations and choices to ensure the entry of reliable data. The current state of ambulatory medical records and the problem of moving reliable data from them into a computerized data base is perhaps the most serious technical barrier to outcomes management.[3]

The technology assessors acknowledge that their work is largely necessitated by a paucity of data on outcomes. Outcomes management can help to circumvent this weakness by creating an opportunity for continuous improvement through a feedback of outcomes. It can be used to assess and, where appropriate, to modify initial standards. Standards, then, are not rigid laws to be followed blindly forever; they are a starting point--data elements and recommendations that respond continually to what is learned from application and subsequent research.[3]

Two Major Initiatives

The crucial element that would link the actions and observations of thousands of health professionals with millions of patients is a massive computerized database. We seek from this data the inhuman capacity of computers to cope with information gathered over time from multiple sources and to provide on-line feedback to a variety of users. We're not expecting a technology that thinks better than human beings. We need a technology that keeps track of more participants and members better than we do. Advances in the use of computers have led data pooling and management initiatives that together have spurred the most rapidly moving yet the most immature science in outcomes management.[3]

One major initiative being undertaken to fill this need is that by the Department of Health and Human Services, through the Health Care Financing Administration (HCFA) and the Public Health Service.

HCFA has several resources to dedicate to accomplishment of its effectiveness initiative, among them unique access to billing and clinical information and expertise in collecting and interpreting such data. With these resources, HCFA is undertaking four types of projects:

- The use of data from the Medicare systems of claims processing and peer review to monitor trends and to assess the effectiveness of specific interventions.

- The development of a data resource center, where files of Medicare data (including those linking Part A and Part B ambulatory data) will be made available for appropriate research by private persons and organizations.

- The funding of clinical research that will permit ongoing evaluation of the comparative appropriateness and effectiveness of various procedures and interventions, such as those carried out by the RAND Corporation, as well as small area analyses involving the American Medical Review Research Center (AMRRC) and Codman Research Group.

- The expansion and connection of Medicare clinical databases with those of the National Cancer Institute (the cancer registry) and the National Institute of Diabetes and Digestive and Kidney Diseases, including the development of methods to adjust clinical outcomes for health status and severity-of-illness as part of the development of a Uniform Clinical Data Set for the collection of information by the PROs.[4]

HCFA sees the assessment of medical effectiveness and the improvement of clinical practice as a four-step process involving monitoring, analysis of variations, assessment of interventions, and feedback and intervention.[4] Recently, approximately $50 million has been recommended for this area for federal fiscal year 1990.

In Step 1, monitoring, an ongoing universal database composed of all Medicare claims is used to characterize the health status of the population involved (all Medicare beneficiaries), monitor the outcomes of various interventions (mortality, morbidity, disability, and cost),and screen for emerging beneficial or adverse trends.

In Step 2, the goal is to describe and define variations in medical care in terms of both practice patterns and outcomes. Such studies may be population-based (e.g., small area analyses) or may examine the effect of certain interventions (e.g., mortality rates after coronary artery bypass surgery).

In Step 3, interventions are assessed. Variation may result from differences in case selection or in the effectiveness of interventions. At present, a pilot project to perform more refined clinical studies is nearing completion. The project links information from Medicare claims with clinical data abstracted from medical records by PROs. Data from eight PROs on six procedures and conditions are being studied (29,000 case records in all). The six procedures and conditions are coronary revascularization, cholecystectomy, prostatectomy, acute myocardial infarction, congestive heart failure, and pulmonary disease.

Step 4 concerns feedback and education. Information produced by the process just described will have limited usefulness unless it reaches physicians. Several approaches could be used for this purpose, possibly concurrently. The PRO system is a natural vehicle, but other entities, including professional societies, journals, medical schools, and the Public Health Service, should also have key roles.[4]

Another major initiative in the area of clinical outcome management concerns the plans of the American Medical Association and the RAND Corporation to develop "clinical practice parameters" for a wide spectrum of patient conditions. This joint initiative may be regarded as a logical outgrowth of the efforts of HCFA to develop a new reimbursement system for physicians' services under Part B of the Medicare Program.

HCFA favors a capitated system of Medicare reimbursement for physician services or, at the very least, tightly constrained service volume caps on any Part B fee schedule developed from a resource-based relative value scale (RBRVS). Top officials at HCFA believe that a Medicare Part B fee schedule without tight caps on the volume of physician services provided would amount to substituting one inflationary system for another (i.e., the current fee-for-service system). Nevertheless, HCFA wants to ensure that Medicare patients' clinical outcomes do not suffer as a result of imposing either a capitated or a tightly volume constrained fee schedule based on a RBRVS system of reimbursement for physicians.

Therefore, clinical practice parameters, i.e., sound alternative diagnostic and therapeutic strategies for managing different patient conditions of varying illness severity that may be demonstrated as being linked to acceptable clinical outcomes, need to be developed and integrated into various reimbursement schemes (e.g., RBRVS, DRGs, etc.). The term "parameters," rather than guidelines, protocols, or standards, is used in this context to indicate that a range of alternative diagnostic and therapeutic management strategies may prove to be linked to acceptable clinical outcomes in patients presenting to physicians with various conditions and differing illness severities. As various medical information systems, including automated medical records systems (e.g., Ulticare(TM)), severity indexing systems (e.g., Medisgroups(TM), Computerized Severity Index(TM), etc.), and clinical decision support systems (sometimes known as "medical artificial intelligence systems," such as DxPlain(TM), the Mycin(TM) series, etc., become increasingly sophisticated and better integrated, with sufficiently large clinical databases to permit the demonstration of statistically significant patient outcome differences,the acceptable parametric range may well steadily narrow.

However, in light of how rapidly medical technology changes, it is improbable that there will ever be a single "best way" to manage each of the virtually endless number of combinations and permutations of patient conditions and illness severities. Nevertheless, the potential for continual electronic transmission of the constantly changing clinical practice parameters to practicing physicians as envisioned by the AMA and the RAND Corporation should greatly improve both severity-adjusted clinical outcomes and the cost-effectiveness of health care delivery in the 1990s and 21st Century.

Chapter 5

Legal Aspects

Will the development of clinical practice parameters flowing from the linkage of different medical interventions to optimal (or at least "acceptable") clinical outcomes result in an increase or a decrease in professional liability litigation?

One of the major goals of the AMA/RAND Corporation venture is to establish ranges of alternative clinical management strategies and decision making pathways, which, if followed in diagnosing and treating patients with different conditions and illness severities, stand the best chance of effecting at least acceptable, if not optimal, medical outcomes.

Both the AMA and the RAND Corporation realize that there will remain, at least for the foreseeable future, a *range* of possible clinical management strategies for diagnosing and treating different patient conditions of varying illness severity. The methodologies currently available to evaluate and determine these "parameters" are not sufficiently sophisticated to permit the conclusion that any one diagnostic and therapeutic pathway is significantly more effective than others within the boundaries of the clinical parameters.

The clinical parameters to be developed are intended to provide helpful guidance to practicing physicians in their clinical decision making. They are not intended, nor would it currently be appropriate for them, to bind physicians in any way. As technological innovation progresses, these parameters will need to be continuously revised and updated. For that reason, it is probably a substantial oversimplification to refer to any of the parameters as standards of care, with clinical practices that do not conform to them being regarded as deviant (i.e., negligent acts or omissions in the medicolegal sense). At most, proof of the current presence and availability of these clinical practice parameters to a practicing physician defendant in a liability action could provide some evidence of failure to comply with acceptable standards of care, if such a physician's behavior fell clearly outside of the boundaries of the parameters without any forthcoming justification for that deviation.

To develop these clinical practice parameters for the full range of patients' possible conditions will be an arduous task. In all probability, the initial parameters will focus upon the most highly utilized, costly, risky, and invasive procedures, such as those already investigated for appropriateness by the RAND Corporation, e.g., coronary artery bypass grafts (CABGs), percutaneous transluminal coronary angioplasties (PTCAs), cardiac catheterizations, and carotid endarterectomies for cerebrovascular disease.

It should be noted that data-based parameters are already being used by major third-party payers. Various commercially available and proprietary software programs are being used both routinely and on a pilot basis as part of innovative medical quality management programs. One excellent example of this is the pioneering work forged between Value Health Sciences, Inc. (a company directed by Rand researcher, Mark Chassin, MD, MPP), and Aetna Life Insurance Company. Value Health Sciences is sharing its software with Aetna (as well as the Blue Cross and Blue Shield Association) to determine the extent of compliance of physicians with the indications for a total of 36 common procedures. This represents the cutting edge of the industry and presages where other purchasers will follow in the 1990s.

To establish practice parameters, it will be necessary to do extensive statistical evaluations of large clinical databases to assess the relative risks involved in doing or not doing these procedures in patients with the broadest possible spectrum of preprocedural clinical findings and potential indications. Some initial efforts at doing this type of analysis may be found in the section "Coronary Revascularization--An Example" in the fourth reference of this chapter.[4]

The types of medical care evaluation systems developed to permit these types of analyses not only will have increasing quality improvement, utilization management, and financial impacts, but also will certainly provide a nutrient broth for legal and ethical debates. Numerous recent court decisions--e.g., *Hughes v. Blue Cross of Northern California*, Col. App. 3d 958 (1988); *Linthicum v. Nationwide Life Insurance*, 723 P2d 675 (Ariz. 1986); *Taylor v. Prudential Insurance Co.*, 775 P2d 1457 (11 Cir. 1985); *Aetna Life Insurance Co. v. Lavioe*, 505 So. 2d 1050 (Ala. 1987); *Wickline v. California*, 183 Col. App. 3d 1175 (1986)--have already demonstrated the response of the legal system. Liability can be established for various utilization review misadventures, such as the payer's failure to investigate before benefit denial, failure to inform beneficiaries of program administrative and clinical policies, and improper design and application of utilization management systems. Thus, it will not be adequate to simply develop systems that are sufficiently grounded in sensitive, reliable, and valid practice data. It will also be necessary to develop operational systems in both health care delivery and reimbursement that have a high degree of quality control to minimize adverse health outcomes and financial risks. Moreover, the challenges that will continue to emanate from various provider risk and incentive mechanisms in managed care systems will be tested at the professional, ethical, and legal levels. Thus, the work that has only just begun in outcome evaluation will be closely monitored by a legal system that is both opportunistic and dedicated to protecting the patient as a value purchaser.

Summary

Both the research in outcome evaluation by HCFA and the development of clinical practice parameters by the AMA and the RAND Corporation are intended, first and foremost, to improve the overall quality of medical care. This is sought in both initiatives through a process of linking various practice patterns associated with the management of different patient conditions and illness severities with acceptable, if not optimal, clinical outcomes. These linkages and parameters will be in a continuous state of flux as technological innovation and the science and art of clinical outcomes management evolve.

Because they present such a "moving target," it is improbable (and probably inappropriate) that these medical interventions linked to acceptable patient outcomes (i.e., clinical practice parameters) should ever be considered as medical or legal standards of care. The development of these practice parameters and adherence to them by a substantial portion of physicians should decrease liability risk and insurance premiums to underwrite it. This has already proved to be the case in Massachusetts, where, by following the Harvard/American Society of Anesthesiologists' clinical practice guidelines, anesthesiologists insured though the Commonwealth's Joint Underwriting Association (JUA) have actually enjoyed a substantial *decrease* in their malpractice premiums as a result of the absence of any successful claims for significant neurologic or cerebral impairment being filed over a recent policy period.[5]

Therefore, it would appear that development of and adherence to clinical practice parameters for the widest possible range of highly utilized, risky, costly and potentially errorprone procedures as soon as possible would not only improve the quality of patient care, but also substantially relieve the currently oppressive malpractice litigation environment.

Conclusion--Looking Ahead

Clinical outcome evaluation and management is clearly a concept and a process whose time has come in the American health care industry. As Paul Ellwood, MD, has said, the health care system is an organization "desperately in need of a central nervous system that can help it cope with the complexities of modern medicine."[3] To the extent that clinical outcome management may serve as the vehicle and process to communicate to practicing physicians the most effective, appropriate, and efficient clinical management of patients with various conditions and illness severities, it may well serve as that "central nervous system."

Clinical outcome evaluation and management is a science and an art, just as the practice of medicine is, and likely always will be. If anything, clinical outcome evaluation and management should help to decrease the amount of "cookbook practice" of medicine. Much of medical education is still geared toward teaching physicians in training to be obsessively compulsive in their ordering of tests, procedures, and consultations for patients with similar clinical presentations but often with very different illness severities and prognoses.

Clinical outcome evaluation and management is intended to provide guidance to practitioners concerning the variable ranges of appropriate clinical decisionmaking in these very different types of patients to *decrease* the unnecessary, inappropriate, wasteful, and often harmful compulsive consumption of scarce medical resources. Rather than increase the risk of litigation, over time, this should decrease the risk of litigation through this decreasing of unnecessary, often misleading, and potentially harmful tests, procedures and hospitalizations. This should also provide more confidence to practitioners, patients, and purchasers alike that only those resources scientifically demonstrated to be useful in improving different types of patients' health status are utilized in an appropriate, effective, and efficient manner. The progressive initiatives by HCFA and the AMA/RAND Corporation joint venture should be given every chance for success.

References

1. Couch, J. *Medical Quality Management for Physician Executives in the 1990s: Essentials of Medical Quality Management*. Tampa, Fla.: American Academy of Medical Directors, 1988, p.6.

2. Couch, J. "Education in Clinical Outcome Management: Who Needs It?" *Quality Assurance and Utilization Review* (to appear August 1989).

3. Ellwood, P. "Shattuck Lecture: Outcomes Management--a Technology of Patient Experience." *New England Journal of Medicine* 318(23):1549-56, June 9, 1988.

4. Roper, W., and others. "Effectiveness in Health Care: An Initiative to Evaluate and Improve Medical Practice. *New England Journal of Medicine* 319(18):1197-202, Nov. 3, 1988.

5. "Society Release Anesthesia and Postanesthesia Care Standards." *Hospital Peer Review* 13(12):157-9, Dec. 1988.

James B. Couch, MD, JD, is a medical quality management consultant to the executive offices of Metropolitan Hospital, Philadelphia, Pennsylvania. He is Vice Chair of the College's Forum on Law and Medicine and represents the College at the Joint Commission on Accreditation of Healthcare Organizations. Alex R. Rodriguez, MD, FACPE, is Senior Vice President, Professional Affairs, Preferred Health Care, Ltd., Wilton, Connecticut. He is Chair of the College's Forum on Quality Health Care.

Chapter Six

Physician Executives as Medical Systems Experts

by James B. Couch, MD, JD

The Importance of Systems

If there is one word that could best describe health care in the 1990s and early 21st century, it would be "systems." The emerging "Information Age," which has already transformed many industries in America, will have the greatest impact on health care in the 1990s and beyond for at least the following reasons:

- It is an industry that is driven primarily by information, both theoretical and practical.

- It is an industry desperately in need of linkages of its many disparate, currently disorganized, and often inconsistent components (e.g., delivery, purchase, supplier, consumer, evaluation, and regulatory components).

- It is an industry that requires the means to access current, accurate, continuously updated information on the latest, most appropriate, effective, and efficient services.

- It is an industry that has come under recent criticism for being largely unmanaged and unaccountable, particularly in view of the tremendous expenditure of public and private sector funds for it.

- It is an industry that by its size alone (15 percent of the GNP, $1.5 trillion, by the year 2000, according to the General Accounting Office) will be disproportionately affected, as *all* American industries become significantly more systematized in the decades ahead.

"In spite of the fact that management is responsible for the system, or for lack of the system, I find in my experience that few people in industry know what constitutes a system. Many people think of machinery and data processing when I mention system. Few of them know that recruitment, training, supervision, and aids to production are part of the system. Who else could be responsible for these activities?"[1]

As the world authority on quality, Deming's indictment of Western management's ignorance concerning what constitutes "systems" is tantamount to an indictment of their ignorance (until recently) about quality--what it is and how to obtain and retain it. Upon moving to Japan after being shunned by his native America 40 years ago, Deming realized then (as American industry has finally been forced to admit) that the key to industrial success is and will be determined by the quality of products and services delivered compared with that of competitors. The quality of these products and services, on the other hand, will be determined primarily by how good the systems are that permit the efficient flow of materials, information, and people through the production process. Thus, industries' economic survival will, in great measure, depend upon how good their systems are that are designed, developed, implemented, and actualized. There is no industry for which this will apply more in the 1990s than the health care industry.

Physician Executives' Evolving Role as Interface Professionals

As Leland Kaiser, Ph.D., has indicated in many of his inspirational speeches, everything in the universe is part of a system. Certainly the health care industry is a very large system composed of innumerable smaller systems. Perhaps the major reason behind this industry's worsening problems of affordability, access, and demonstrable effectiveness relates to its failure to integrate its various types of systems: medical records systems, nursing acuity systems, physician ordering systems, pharmaceutical systems, insurance systems, billing systems, cost accounting systems, severity indexing systems, among others. Never has the need to integrate these systems (particularly financial and clinical systems) been greater in the health care setting.

There is no other professional more ideally suited to begin to effect the integration of health care clinical and financial systems than physician executives. Their general training in the theory and practice of medicine, as well as specific training in the organization and effective management of health care delivery institutions, puts them at the interface of the two systems that must be integrated to ensure the provision of effective, yet affordable, medical care in the future.

The question remains, however: Is there any common medium through which the necessary integration of these two major types of systems might be facilitated? As strange as it may seem, the legal system, which so often has proved to be a costly obstacle to systematic change, may well be that common medium.

The Legal System as an Agent of Systematic Change in the Health Care Industry

Because of the constant threat of costly, emotionally draining litigation, professionals, especially in the health care industry, recently have assumed an overly cautious stance whenever confronted with environmental forces pressing for systemic change. This is one of the great tragedies of the late 20th century. Legal systems must be restructured to facilitate rapid change in response to and in anticipation of evolving environmental forces of national and global scope. Acknowledgment of how and why systems break down should provide the knowledge necessary to design and implement increasingly sophisticated systems that may minimize the risk of adverse occurrences and reactionary litigation. This must be the high road that America takes into the 21st century, if it is to remain a leading economic force in the emerging global marketplace.

Both clinical and financial systems are governed by policies and procedures and rules and regulations that form the common thread between the systems. However, what must occur in the health care industry is a coalescence of both clinical and financial systems policies around the common theme and goal of improving the overall quality and cost-effectiveness of health care delivery. Such a coalescence will not occur in the absence of professionals specifically trained in understanding and integrating both types of systems and knowledgeable about and experienced with legal and regulatory affairs to fashion and enforce the kinds of policies in both systems that promote the ultimate goal of quality improvement. Success in achieving this will depend not so much on physician executives' fund of knowledge in clinical and financial systems and the regulatory process, as it will on their peculiar and invaluable mental faculties for assimilating, accommodating, incorporating, and integrating the apparent inconsistencies and incongruities of the two systems driving health care into the 21st century. The development and refinement of this mindset will be much more critical to the physician leader of the future than will be his or her clinical, research, teaching, or even political expertise, although some exposure to and/or deep appreciation of all of these areas will continue to be important.

Preparation for Physician Executives

There currently is no formal curriculum for physician executives that will turn them into the kind of medical systems experts necessary for tomorrow's health care industry. This author has presented at least one approach in another monograph on medical quality management, as well as in a recently published article.[2,3] Perhaps the most important educational background to have for the eventual development of the required expertise is in philosophy. The mind trained in philosophy is experienced in assimilating, organizing, analyzing, and synthesizing seemingly incongruous, often antithetical and inconsistent, constantly evolving assumptions about the essential nature of abstract concepts. At its heart, medicine, like philosophy (and law), is a social and behavioral science in the sense that it is so strongly influenced by the constantly evolving standards and values in our ever-changing world. To the extent that physician executives learn to appreciate that, they, and the health care industry, will be the better for it.

References

1. Deming, W. *Out of the Crisis*. p. 366. Cambridge, Mass.: Massachusetts Institute of Technology, 1986.

2. Couch, J. *Medical Quality Management for Physician Executives in the 1990's: The Era of Medical Care Value Purchasing*. Tampa, Florida: American College of Physician Executives, 1989.

3. Couch, J., and Radkowsky, A. "Medical Management Education for Medical Students." *Physician Executive* 15(4):25-28, July-Aug. 1989.

James B. Couch, MD, JD, is a medical quality management consultant to the executive offices of Metropolitan Hospital, Philadelphia, Pennsylvania. He is Vice Chair of the College's Forum on Law and Medicine and represents the College at the Joint Commission on Accreditation of Healthcare Organizations.

Chapter Seven

Epilogue

by James B. Couch, MD, JD

This monograph is an outgrowth of the compilation by this author of a three-monograph series entitled *Medical Quality Management for Physician Executives in the 1990's*, published by the American College of Physician Executives. It is intended to focus upon what is potentially both the greatest strength and the greatest weakness in the emerging era of medical quality management, i.e., its legal aspects and implications.

The legal aspects are a source of strength in the medical quality management process to the extent that they provide structure, orderliness, and parameters of acceptability and fairness. These same legal aspects may, however, act to subvert the whole medical quality management process if its participants become so tied down by regulations and paranoid of legal repercussion that they cannot take the necessary and bold, yet measured, steps forward so that the whole science and art of the field may progress. Clearly, this may be the case in the areas covered by chapters 1 and 4, and, in a structural context, in chapters 2 and 3.

As good a method as any for effectively addressing the growing mountain of regulations affecting the delivery and purchasing of medical care is to accept what is beyond control (laws, statutes, regulations, court decisions, etc.), to try to change what still may be changed (pending legislation or regulations, legally risky situations, etc.), and to be wise enough to know the difference. Doing this alone could ameliorate a lot of the stress and acrimony, which is eroding the very foundation of the health care industry.

Chapters 2 and 3 concern how the legal system distributes power through the creation of responsive (and ideally responsible) institutional structures. Chapter 2 dealt with the distribution of power between a hospital and its medical staff. Chapter 3 dealt with the distribution of power within the medical staff to carry out its delegated medical quality management function. However, what is far more important in the health care industry, as we enter the 1990s, concerns not how power is distributed in a hospital or its medical staff, but rather how effectively that power is shared and used for the benefit of patients and to preserve the hospital's ability to compete in the rapidly emerging medical care value purchasing marketplace.[1] To the extent that external regulations, such as the JCAHO's proposed "Hospital Leadership" chapter in its accreditation manual, may effect this integration of the interdependent components in a health care setting, it will have provided a valuable service to the health care industry and all the institutions and providers within it.

The context of Chapter 5 provides a sterling example of how the development and implementation of scientifically derived parameters or ranges of advisable or acceptable conduct may substantially improve a system that is otherwise largely chaotic, as long as those parameters are not oversold or reacted to as inflexible standards or cookbook formulas. Finally, Chapter 6 more explicitly examines how the broad constructs within which the legal system operates may be applied to the health care industry to permit the kind of utilization of its divergent, yet indispensable, components that will be necessary to its economic viability in the 21st Century.

References

1. Couch, J. *Medical Quality Management for Physician Executives in the 1990s: The Era of Medical Care Value Purchasing.* Tampa, Florida: American College of Physician Executives, 1989.

James B. Couch, MD, JD, is a medical quality management consultant to the executive offices of Metropolitan Hospital, Philadelphia, Pennsylvania. He is Vice Chair of the College's Forum on Law and Medicine and represents the College at the Joint Commission on Accreditation of Healthcare Organizations.

Index

A
Accreditation Manual for Hospitals 14
Adequate notice 30
Adverse patient occurrences 17
Aetna Life Insurance Co. 44
Aetna Life Insurance Co. v. Lavoie 44
Agenda for Change 17
American College of Physicians 2,39
American Medical Association 5,39,41,42,43
American Medical Review Research Center 40
Antitrust immunity 3
Antitrust laws 33
Antitrust liability 12
Apparent agency 8
Ascherman v. San Francisco Medical Society 27

B
Bing v. Thunig 25
Blood usage 19
Bolt v. Halifax Hospital Medical Center 36
Bricker v. Sceva Speare Memorial Hospital 27

C
Capitation 42
Charitable immunity 24
Chrisihil v. Annapolis Emergency Hospital Association, Inc. 26,30
Citta v. Delaware Valley Hospital 29
Clinical decision-making 2,42,43
Clinical outcome 42
Clinical parameters 44
Clinical performance profiling 32
Clinical practice parameters 41
Clinical practice guidelines 45
Clinical privileges 13
Clinical standards 44
Codman Research Group 5,40
Computerized Severity Index 42
Conditional accreditation 4
Conditions of Participation, Medicare 4
Contractual liability 8
Corleto v. Shore Memorial Hospital 7,25
Corporate liability 7,25
Council of Medical Specialty Societies 39
Credentialing 2,20,25,26,28,29,32

D
Darling v. Charleston Community Hospital 7,25
Decision-making, clinical 2,42,43
Dillard v. Rowland 28
Disaster plans 19
Discipline, physician 3
Doctrine of state action 36
Dos-Santos v. Columbus-Cuneo-Cabrini Medical Center 34
Due process 26,27,29,31
DxPlain 42

E
Elam V. College Park Hospital 7,25
Exclusive agreements 34
Exclusive contracts 35

F
Foster v. Mobile County Hospital Board 29

Index

G
Garrow v. Elizabeth General Hospital and Dispensary 27,30
Gonzalez v. Nork 25
Griesman v. Newcomb Hospital 27
Group boycotts 33,34,35

H
Hayman v. Galveston 26
Health Care Financing Administration 4,5,40
Health Care Quality Improvement Act 3,29,30,31
Health Resources Services Administration 3
Holmes v. Hoemako Hospital 33
Hospital accreditation 4
Hospital governing board 15
Hughes v. Blue Cross of Northern California 44

I
Immunity, antitrust 3
Independent contractors 24,25
Infection control 19,21
Information Age 48
Institute of Medicine 39

J
JCAHO Standards 11
Jefferson Parish Hospital District No. 2 v. Hyde 34
John Wennberg 5
Johnson v. Misericordia Hospital 26
Joint Commission on Accreditation of Healthcare Organizations 4,11,12,14,17,26,29,32,
Joyce Craddick, MD 17
Judicial review 27

K
Kennedy v. St. Joseph Memorial Hospital of Kokomo, Indiana, Inc. 32
Klinge v. Lutheran Charities Association of St. Louis 31

L
Leland Kaiser, PhD 49
Liability 7,45
Licensure 2
Linthicum v. Nationwide Life Insurance 44

M
Medical information systems 42
Medical Management Analysis system 17
Medical records 19,21
Medical records systems 42
Medical staff bylaws 12
Medical staff clinical departments 18
Medical staff committee structure 18
Medical staff definition 11
Medical staff Executive Committee 18
Medical staff functions 15
Medical staff legal status 11
Medical staff, quality assurance 15
Medical staff responsibilities 13
Medical staff self-governance 12
Medicare 41
Medicare Conditions of Participation 4,29
Medicare Risk Contracts 5
Medisgroups 42
Mycin 42

N
National Cancer Institute 41
National Institutes of Health 39

55

National Institute of Diabetes and Digestive and Kidney Diseases 41
National Practitioner Data Bank 3
North Broward Hospital District v. Mizell 29

O
Occurrence screening 17
Omnibus Budget Reconciliation Act 5
Outcome assessment 4,5,17,45
Outcome management 38,45

P
Park Hospital District v. District Court 30
Patrick v. Burget 35
Paul Ellwood, MD 45
Peer review 26,30,36
Peer review confidentiality 30
Peer Review Improvement Act 5
Peer review organizations 5
Per se rule 33
Pharmacy and therapeutics 19
Physician credentialing 2
Physician discipline 3
Physician executive, quality role 21
Physician reimbursement 42
Physician rights 26
Practice parameters 44
Privileges 3,26,28,32,33
PROs 41
Public Health Service 40

Q
Quality assessment 39
Quality, definition 6

R
RAND Corp. 40,41,42,43
RAND/UCLA Group 5
Reimbursement 42

Resource-based relative value scale 42
Respondeat superior 7,8,24
Restraint of trade 26
Restriction of privileges 3,26,29
Review function committee 18
Risk management 19,20,21
Rule of reason 33

S
Safety 19
Severity-of-illness adjustments 41
Sherman Antitrust Act 35
Silver v. Castle Memorial Hospital 30
Surgical case review 18

T
Tax Equity and Fiscal Responsibility Act 5
Taylor v. Prudential Insurance Co. 44
Technology assessment 39
Third-party beneficiary 8

U
Ulticare 42
Uniform Clinical Data Set 41
Utilization review 19,21

V
Value Health Sciences 44
Vicarious liability 7,24

W
Weiss v. York Hospital 29,35
Wickline v. State of California 7,44
Woodward v. Porter Hospital 27